PIANO SOLO

MOVIE CLASSICS FOR PIANO

CONTENTS

ISBN 978-0-7935-9510-5

Hal•Leonard®
CORPORATION

7777 W. BLUEMOUND RD. P.O. BOX 13819 MILWAUKEE, WI 53213

Visit Hal Leonard Online at
www.halleonard.com

CAVATINA
from the Universal Pictures and EMI Films Presentation THE DEER HUNTER

By STANLEY MYERS

Slowly with feeling

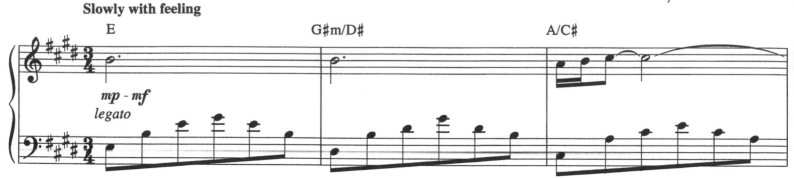

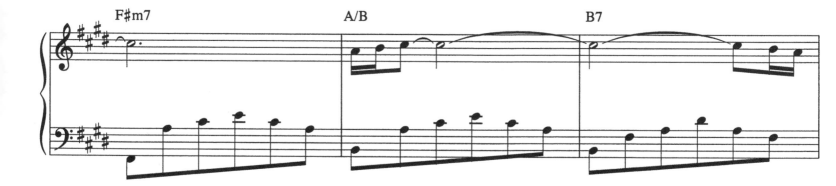

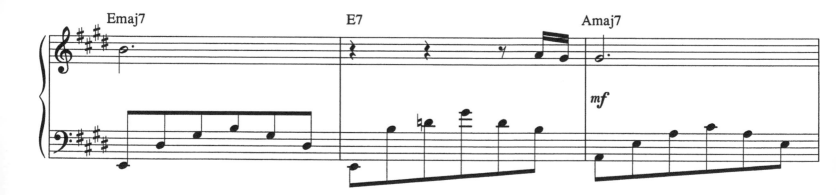

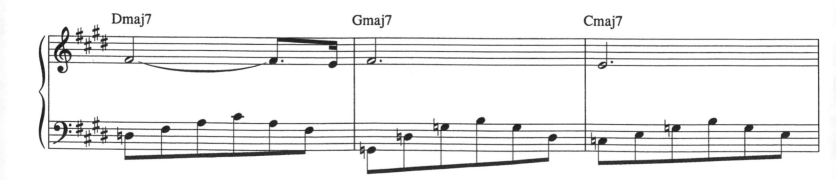

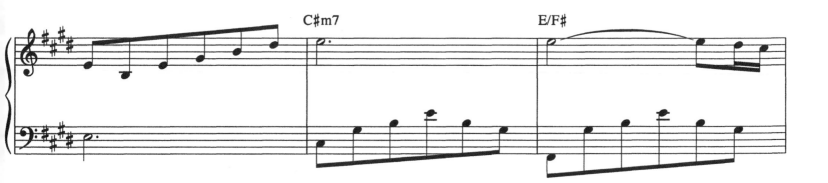

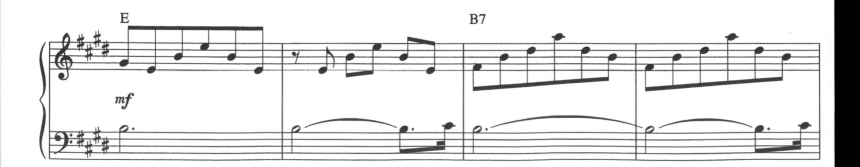

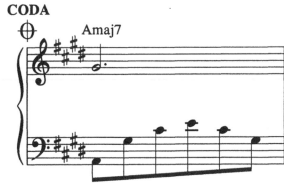

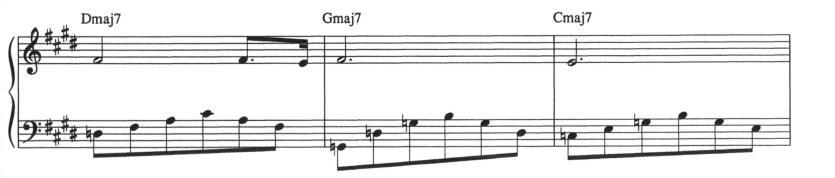

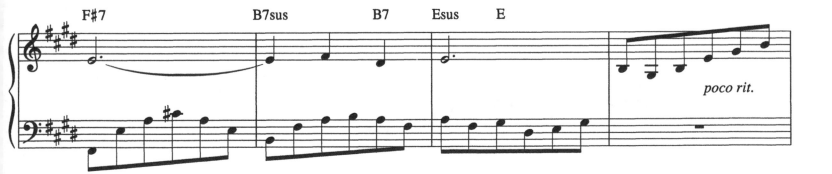

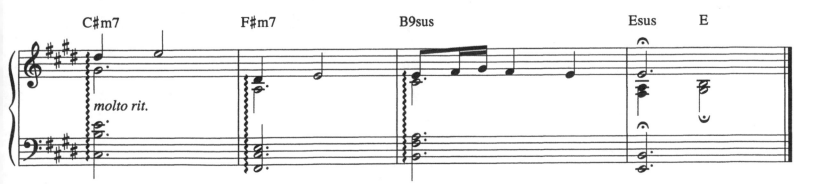

CHARIOTS OF FIRE
from CHARIOTS OF FIRE

Music by VANGELIS

Moderately

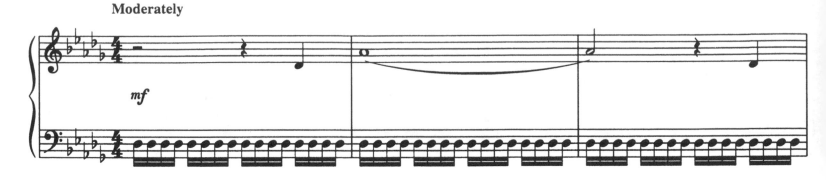

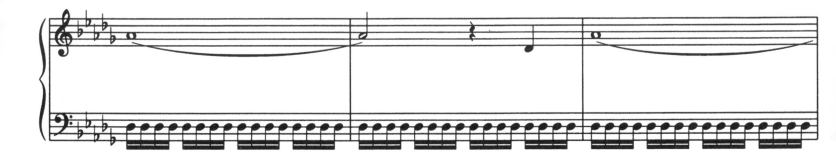

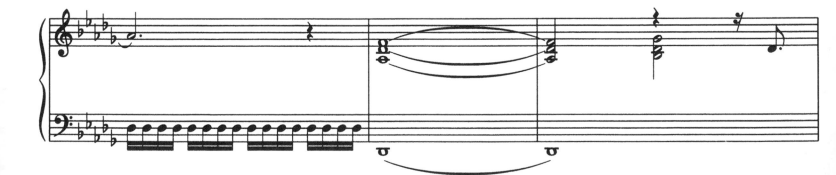

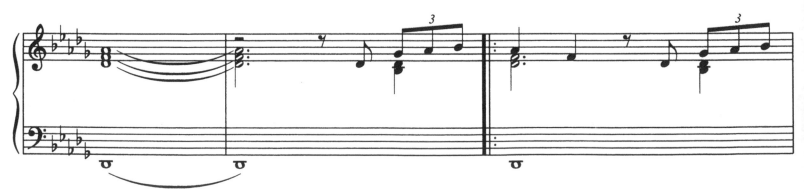

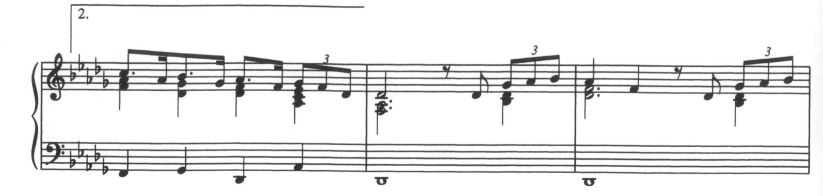

ADAGIO FOR STRINGS
from PLATOON

By SAMUEL BARBER

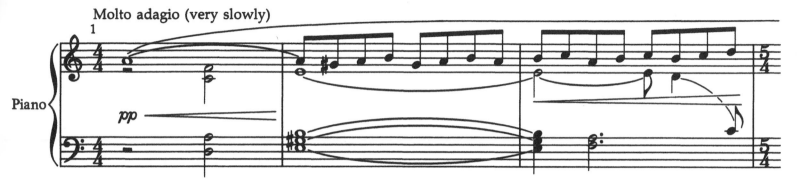

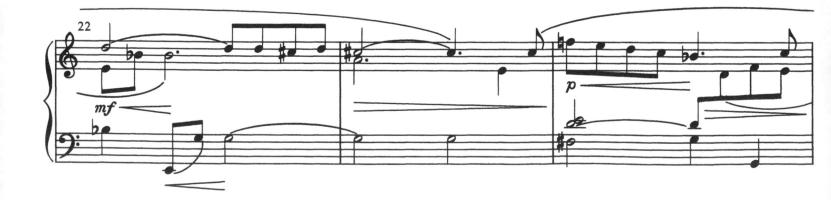

(with increasing intensity)

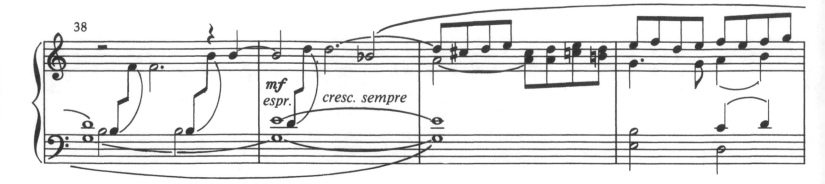

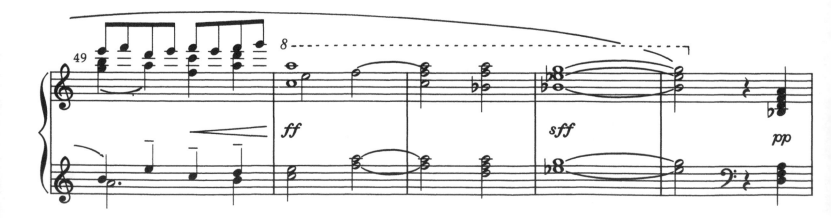

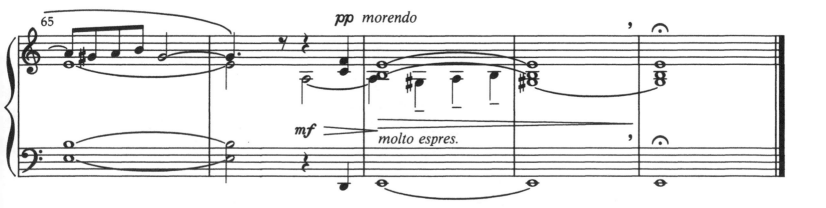

CONVENTO DI SANT' ANNA
from THE ENGLISH PATIENT

Written by GABRIEL YARED

Slowly, but steadily

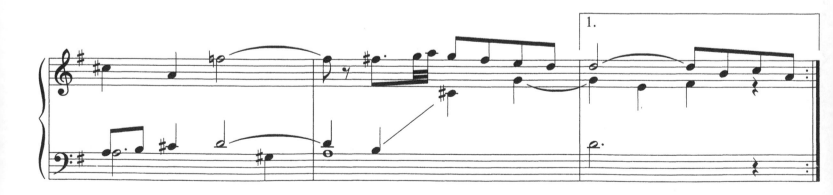

To Coda ⊕

more deliberately

tempo one

D.S. al Coda

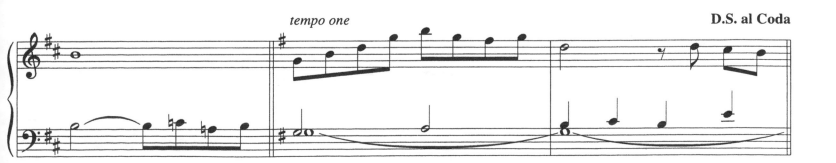

18

CODA

THE ENGLISH PATIENT
from THE ENGLISH PATIENT

Written by GABRIEL YARED

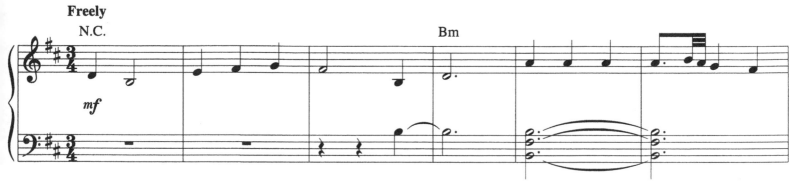

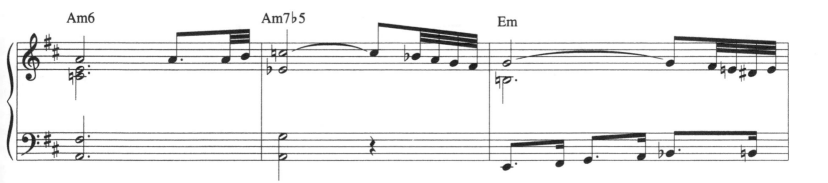

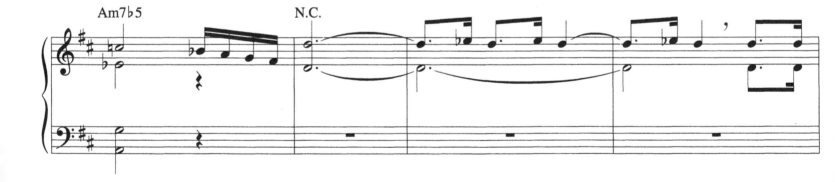

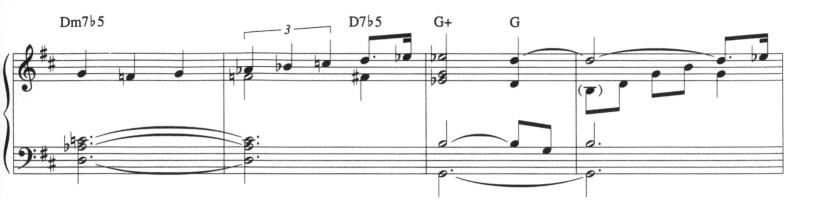

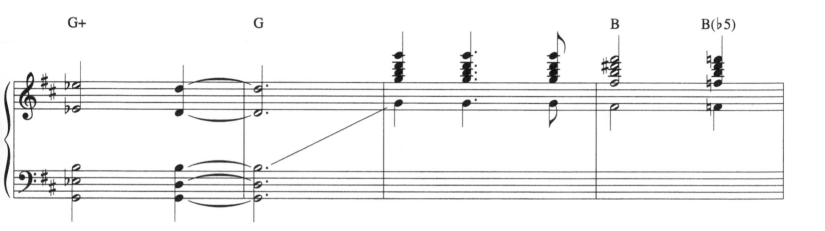

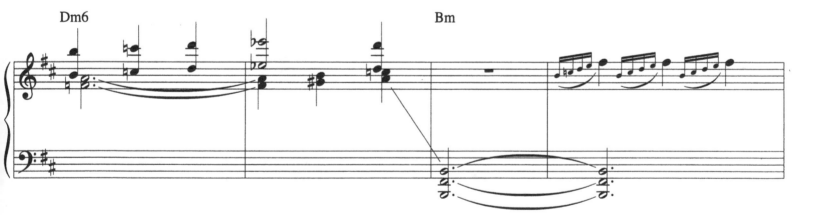

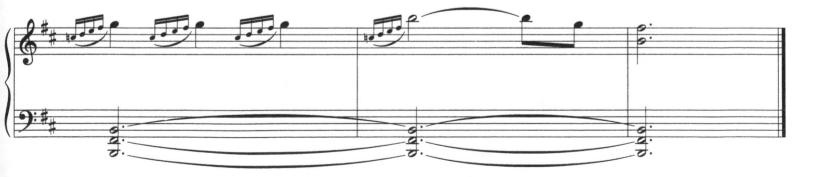

DON'T CRY FOR ME ARGENTINA

from EVITA

Words by TIM RICE
Music by ANDREW LLOYD WEBBER

Freely

Moderately slow, rhythmic

MCA Music Publishing

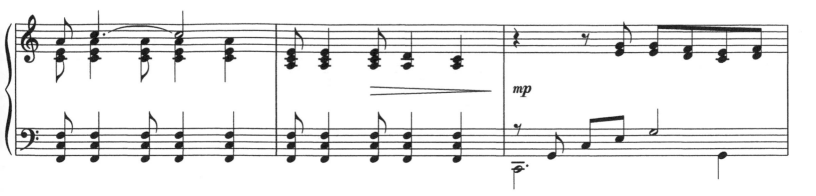

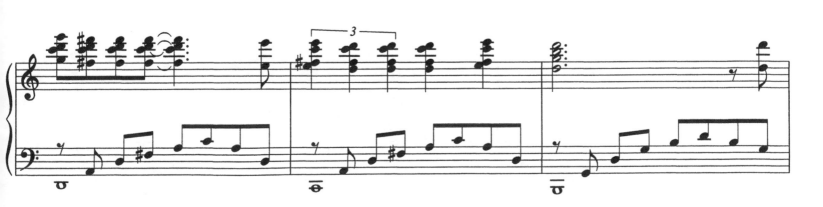

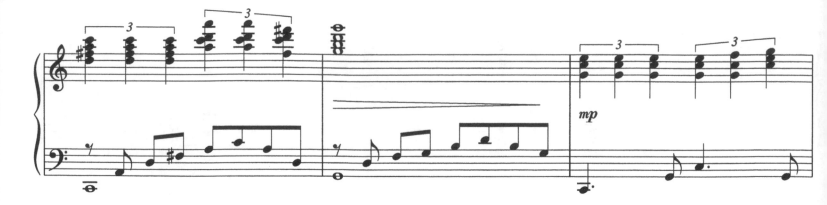

THE EXODUS SONG

from EXODUS

Words by PAT BOONE
Music by ERNEST GOLD

Slowly and expressively

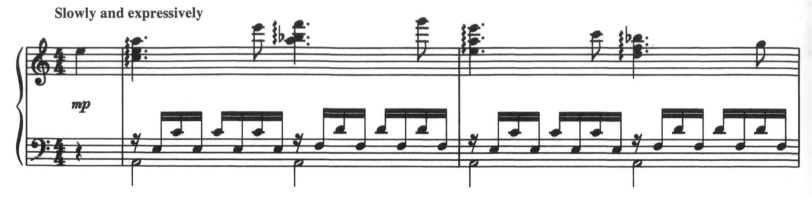

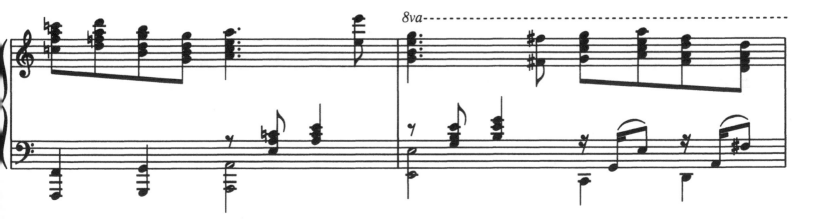

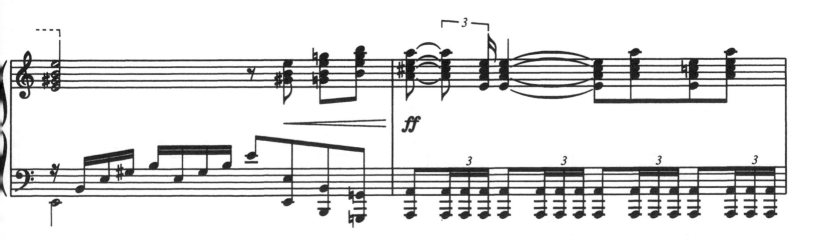

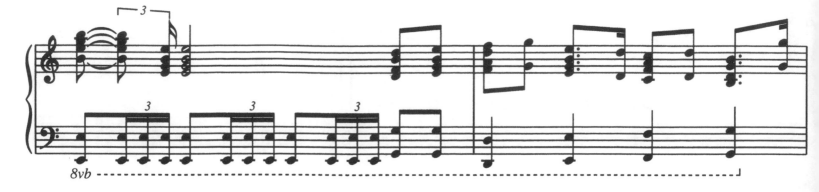

THE GODFATHER
(LOVE THEME)
from the Paramount Picture THE GODFATHER

By NINO ROTA

Slowly and expressively

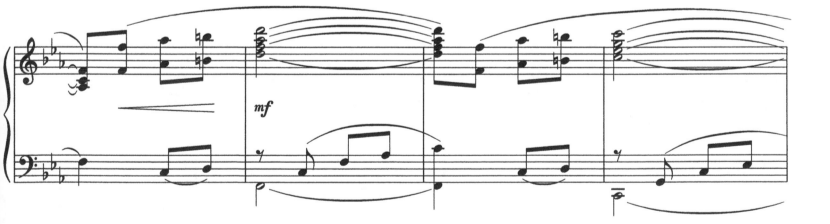

FORREST GUMP - MAIN TITLE
(FEATHER THEME)
from the Paramount Motion Picture FORREST GUMP

Music by ALAN SILVESTRI

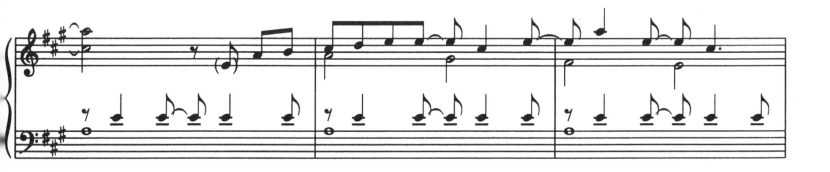

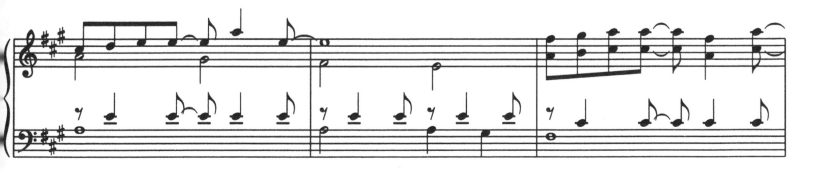

_8va_

(lightly)

f

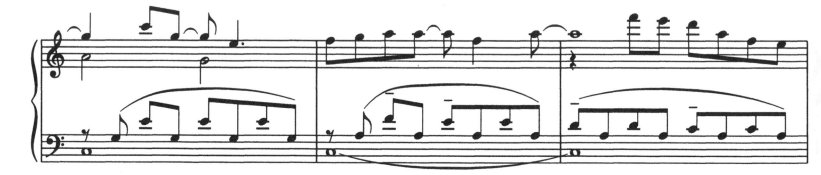

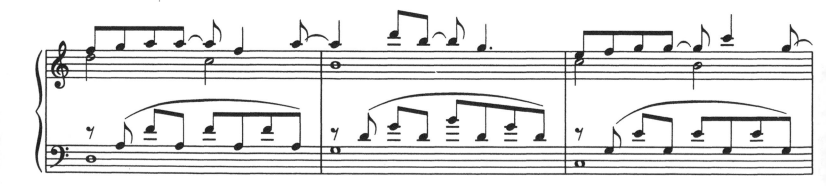

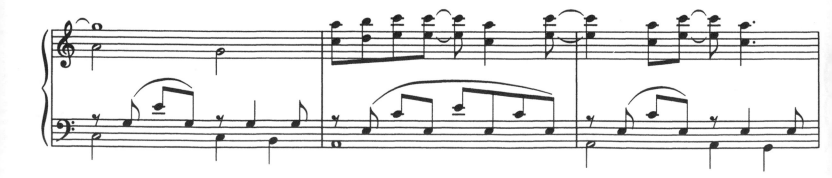

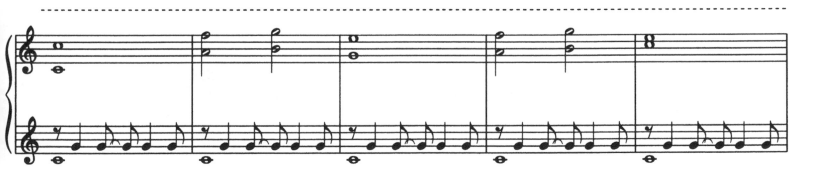

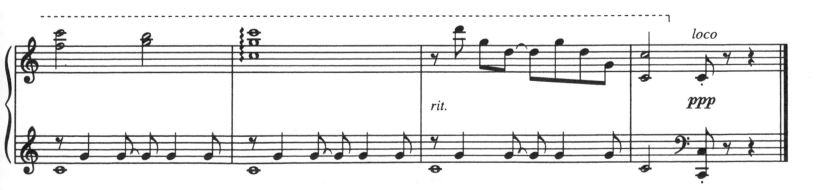

THE JOHN DUNBAR THEME
from DANCES WITH WOLVES

By JOHN BARRY

Moderately

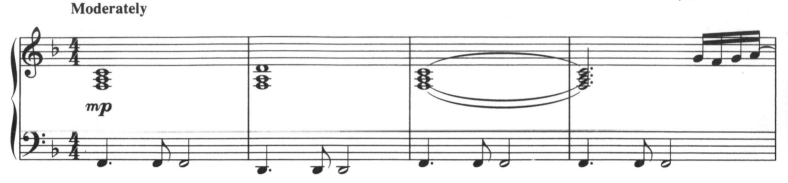

To Coda ⊕

(End opt. 8va)

D.S. al Coda

CODA

THEME FROM "JURASSIC PARK"

from the Universal Motion Picture JURASSIC PARK

Composed by JOHN WILLIAMS

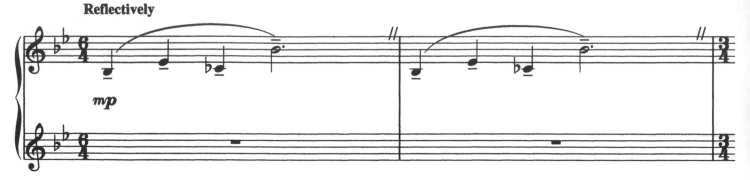

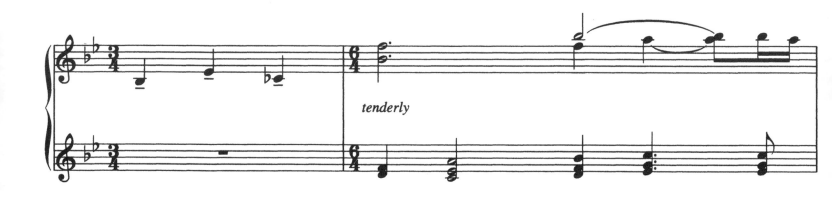

LEGENDS OF THE FALL
from TriStar Pictures' LEGENDS OF THE FALL

Composed by JAMES HORNER

Tempo I

THEME FROM "THE LOST WORLD"

from the Universal Motion Picture THE LOST WORLD: JURASSIC PARK

Composed by
JOHN WILLIAMS

Forcefully

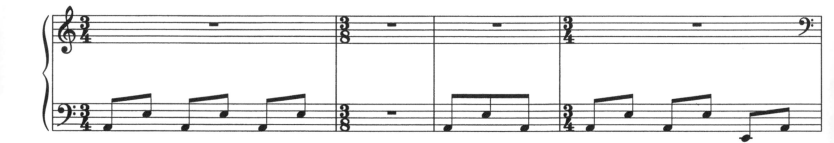

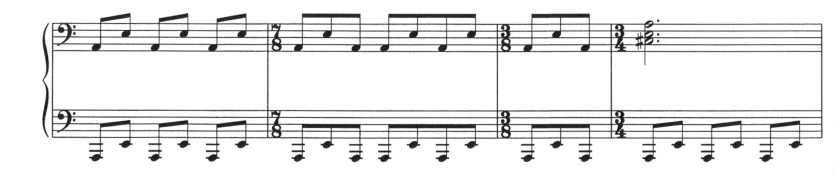

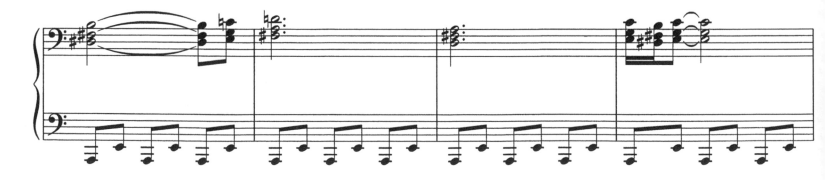

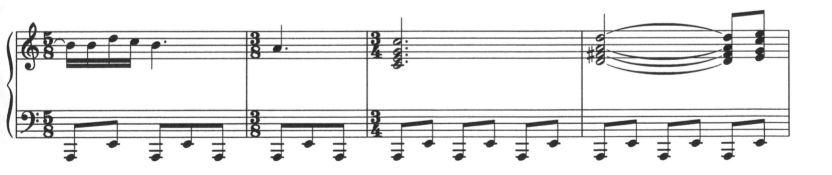

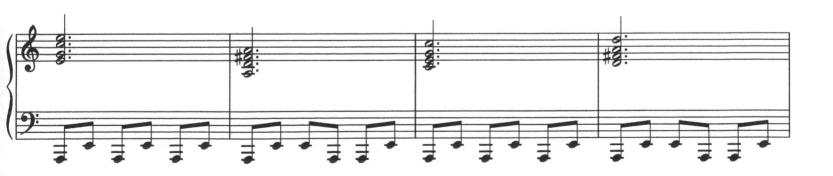

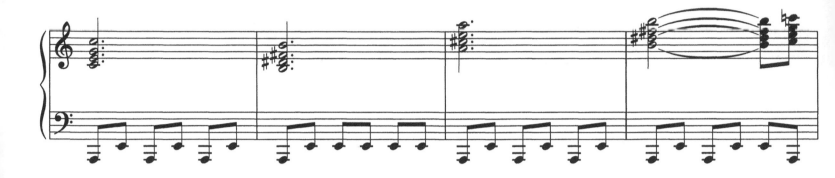

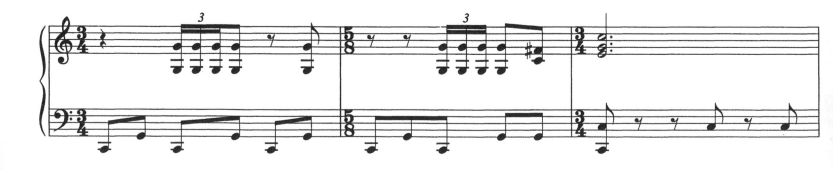

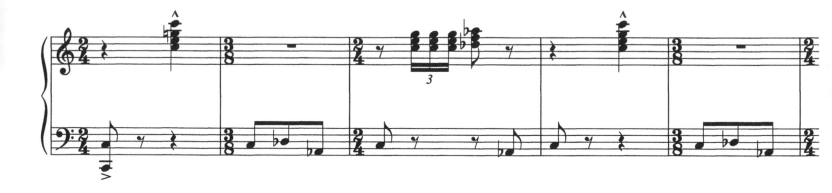

ON GOLDEN POND
Main Theme from ON GOLDEN POND

Music by DAVE GRUSIN

Very freely

p very delicately, as though from far away

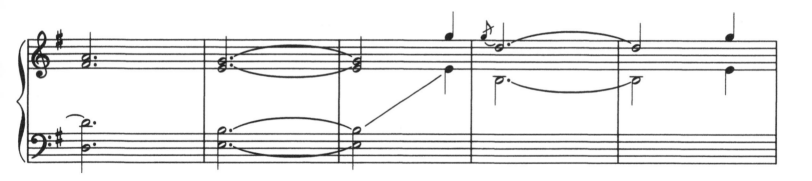

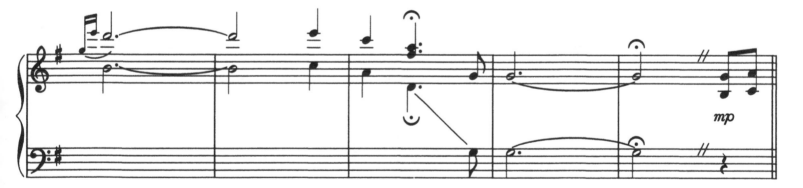

Andante rubato*

*Not fast and somewhat freely

Ped.

8va - - - - - - - - - - - - - -

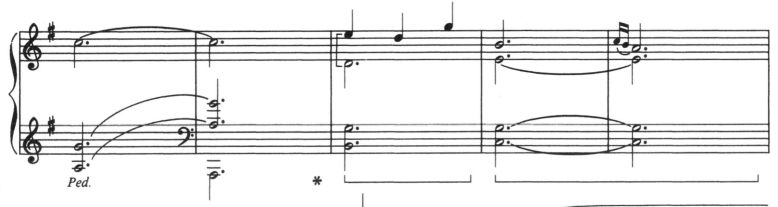

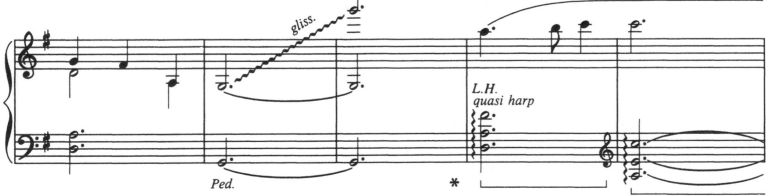

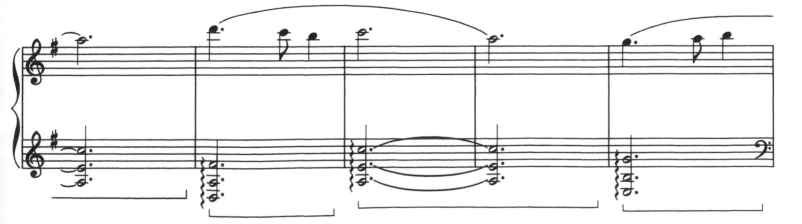

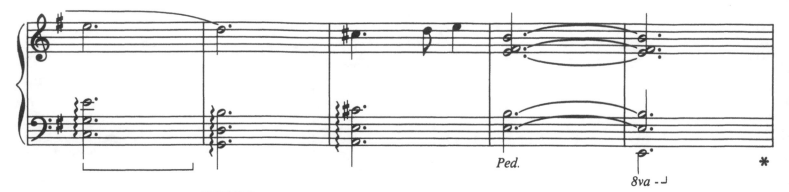

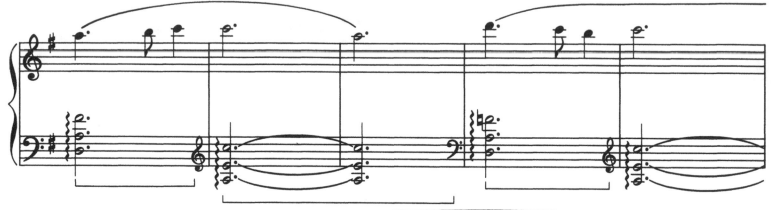

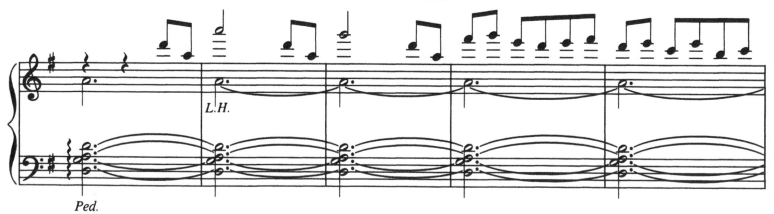

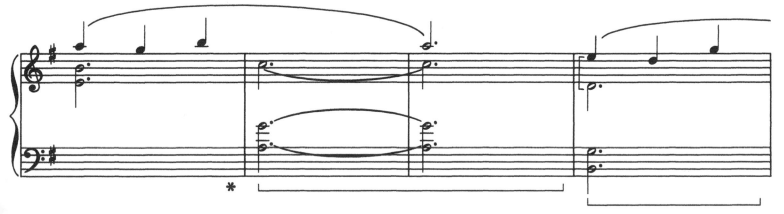

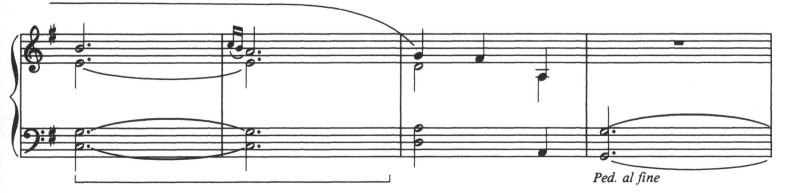

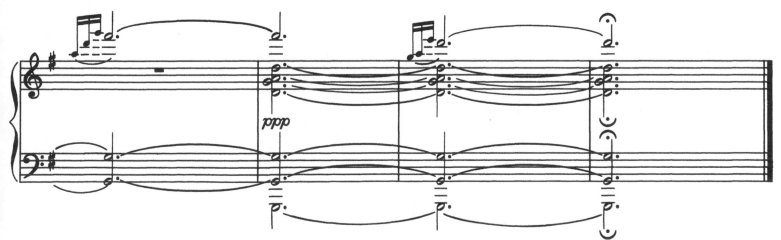

LOVE STORY
Theme from the Paramount Picture LOVE STORY

Music by FRANCIS LAI

Slowly, expressively

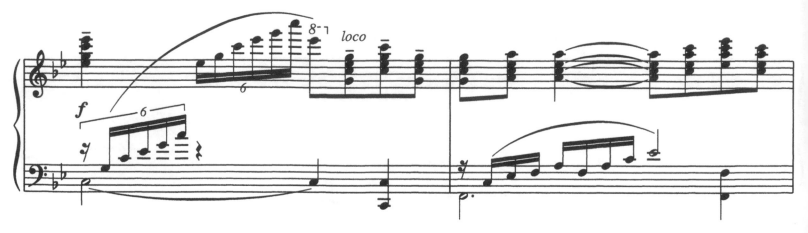

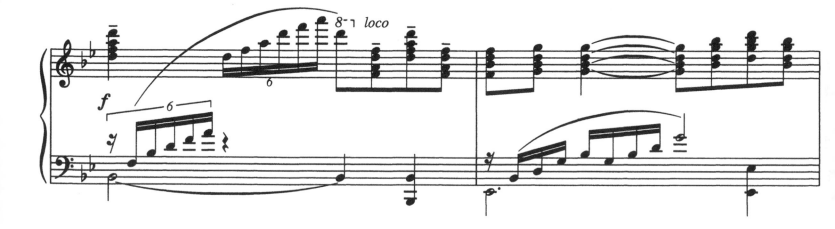

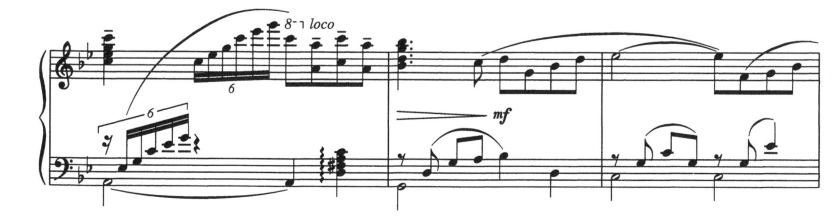

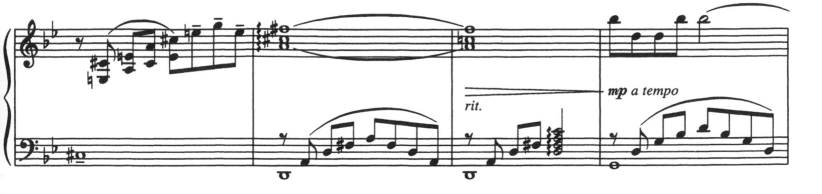

THE MAN FROM SNOWY RIVER
(MAIN TITLE THEME)
from THE MAN FROM SNOWY RIVER

By BRUCE ROWLAND

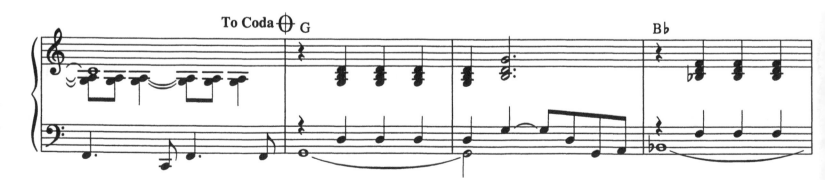

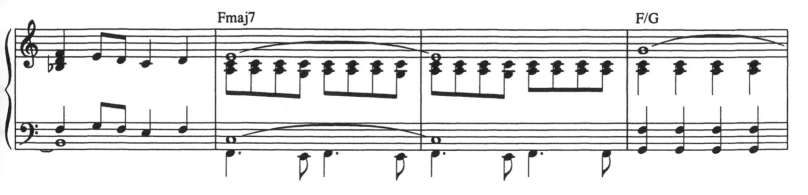

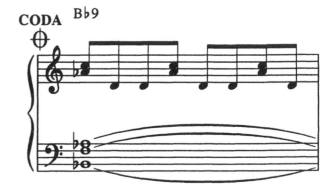

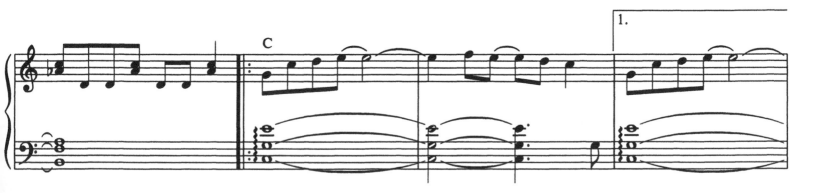

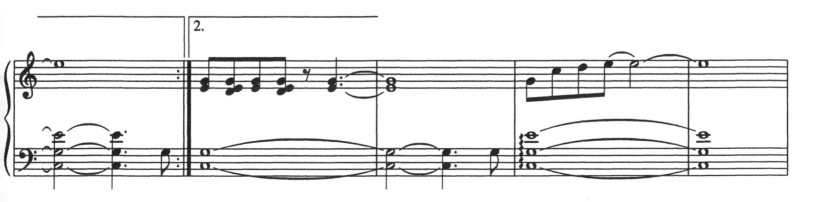

MISSION: IMPOSSIBLE THEME

from the Paramount Motion Picture MISSION: IMPOSSIBLE

By LALO SCHIFRIN

Moderately, with drive

MY FATHER'S FAVORITE

from SENSE AND SENSIBILITY

By PATRICK DOYLE

Andante cantabile

MY HEART WILL GO ON
(LOVE THEME FROM 'TITANIC')
from the Paramount and Twentieth Century Fox Motion Picture TITANIC

Music by JAMES HORNER
Lyric by WILL JENNINGS

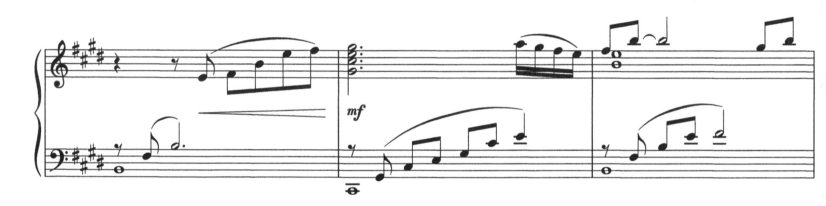

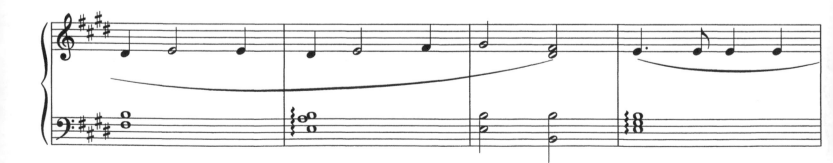

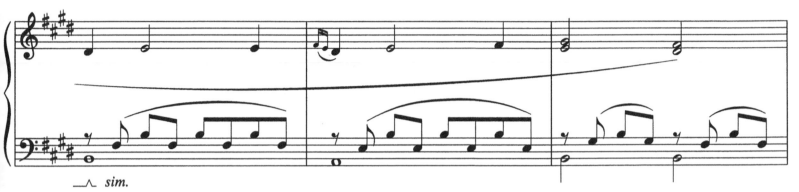

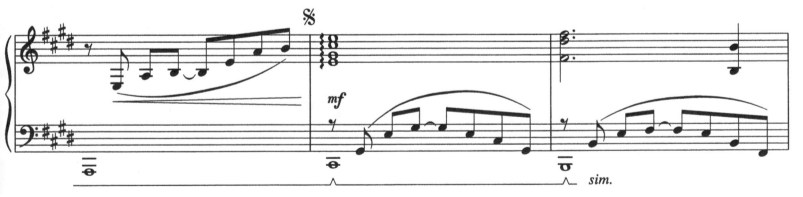

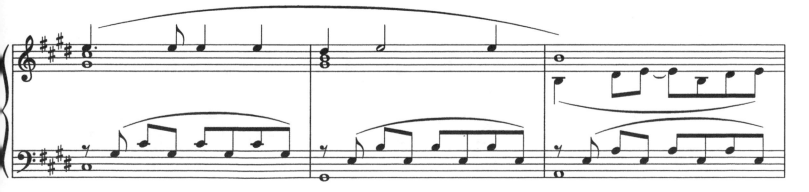

D.S. al Coda

CODA

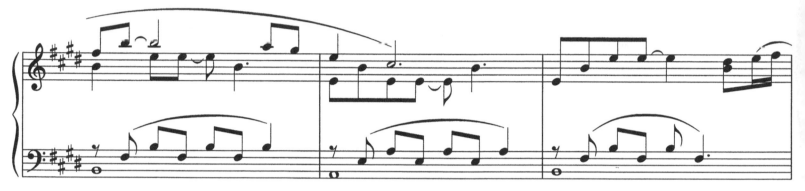

broaden

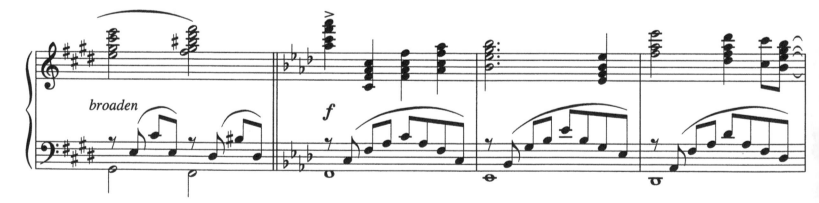

LOVE THEME FROM "OUT OF AFRICA"
(THE MUSIC OF GOODBYE)
from OUT OF AFRICA

Music by JOHN BARRY
Words by ALAN and MARILYN BERGMAN

Slowly

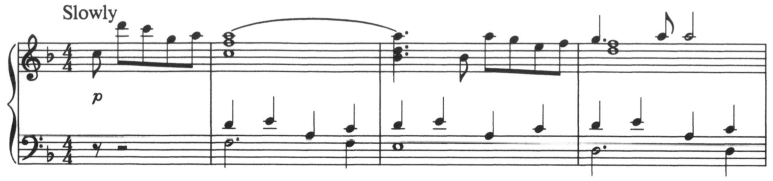

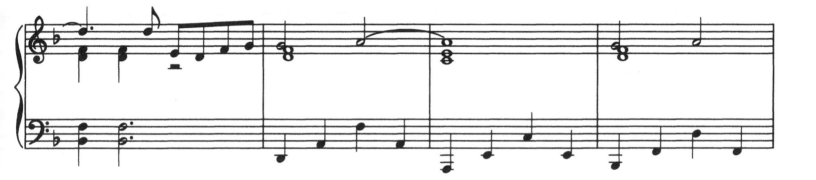

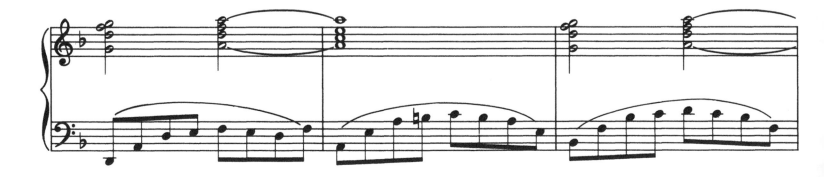

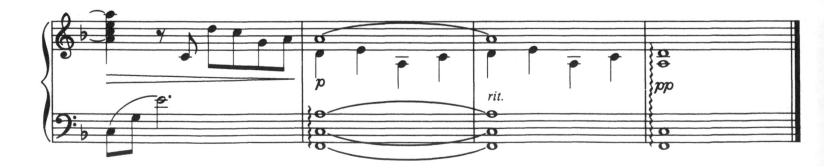

ROMEO AND JULIET
(LOVE THEME)
from the Paramount Picture ROMEO AND JULIET

By NINO ROTA

Slowly, poignantly

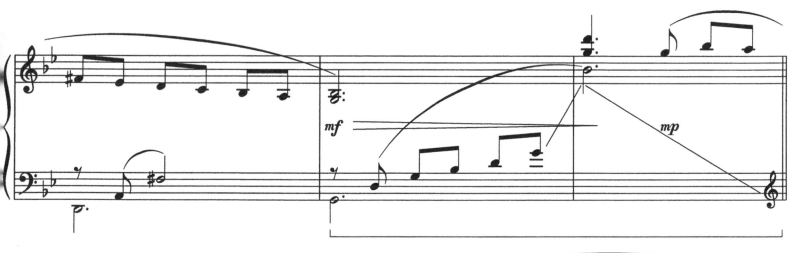

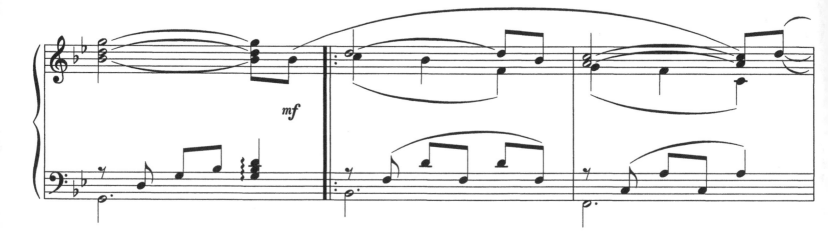

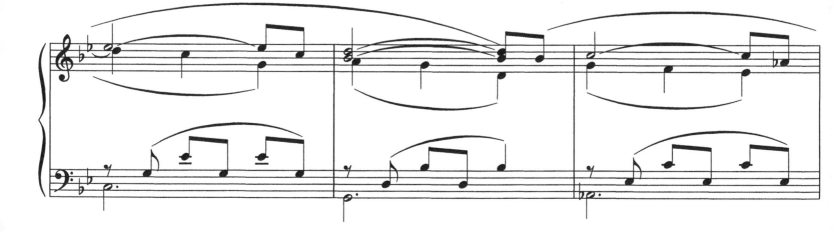

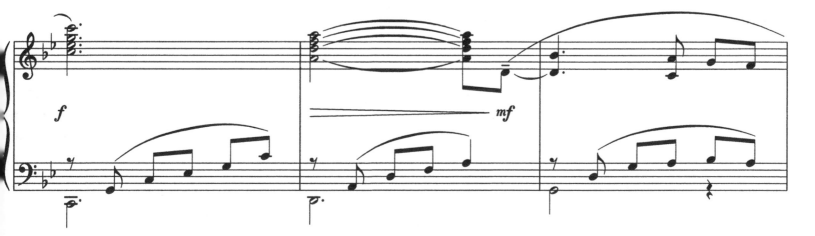

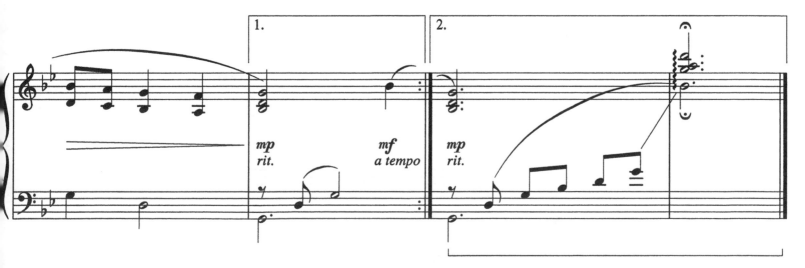

RAIDERS MARCH
from the Paramount Motion Picture RAIDERS OF THE LOST ARK

Music by JOHN WILLIAMS

March tempo

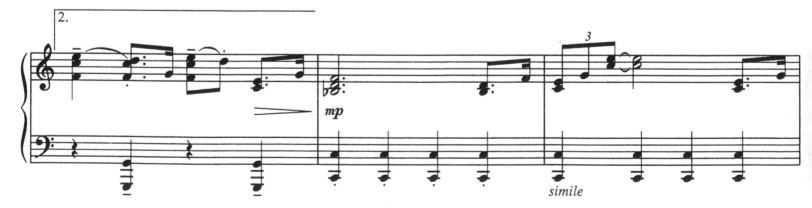

sim.

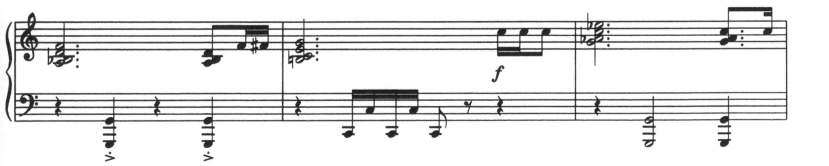

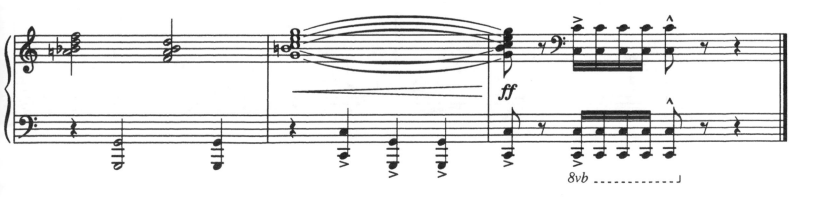

THEME FROM "SABRINA"
from the Paramount Motion Picture SABRINA

By JOHN WILLIAMS

More movement

legato

cresc.

poco rit.

f espressivo

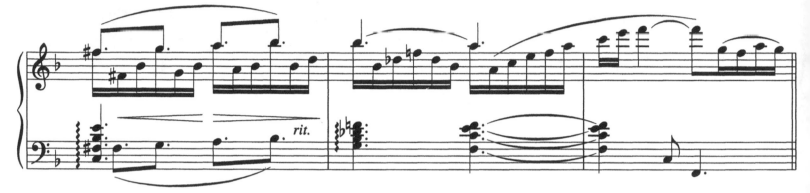

Tempo I

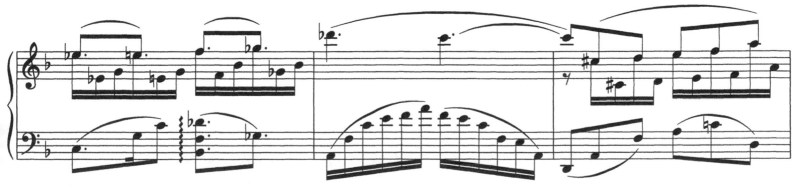

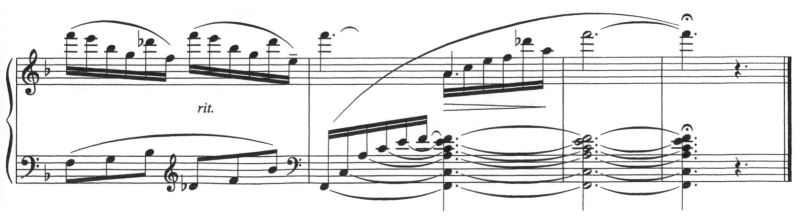

THEME FROM "SCHINDLER'S LIST"

from the Universal Motion Picture SCHINDLER'S LIST

Composed by JOHN WILLIAMS

SOMEWHERE IN TIME

from SOMEWHERE IN TIME

By JOHN BARRY

THEME FROM
"TERMS OF ENDEARMENT"

from the Paramount Picture TERMS OF ENDEARMENT

By MICHAEL GORE

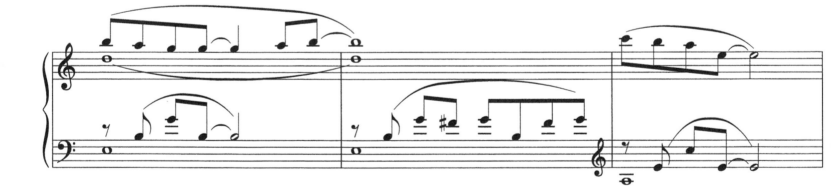

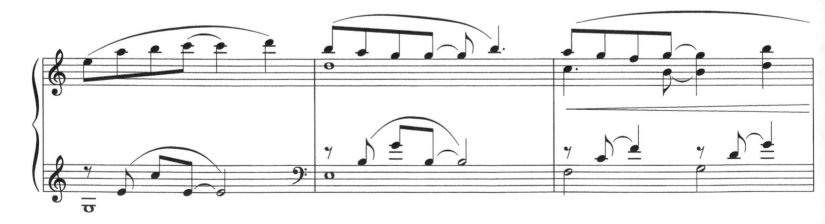

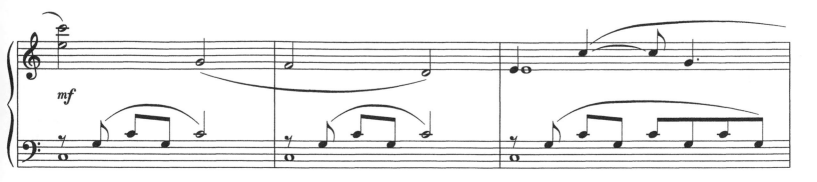

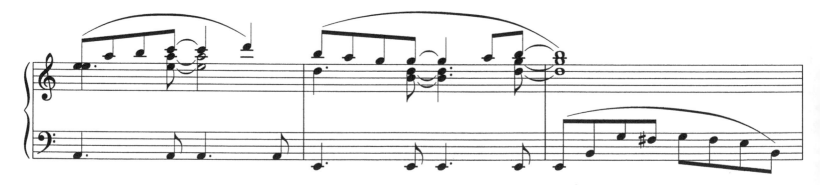

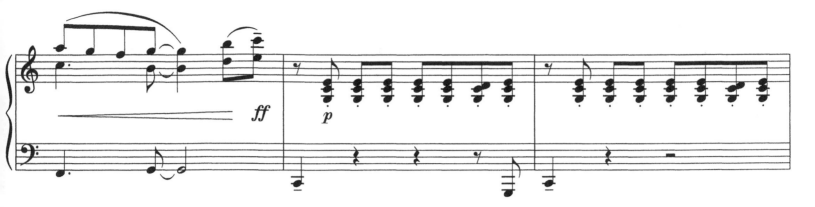

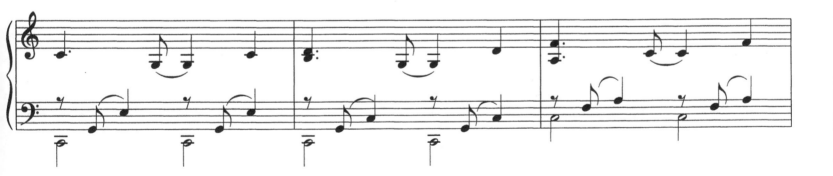

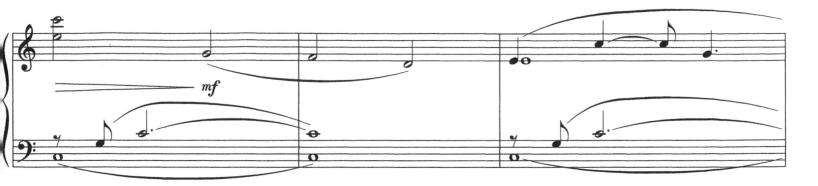

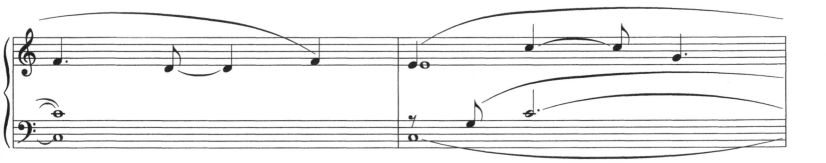

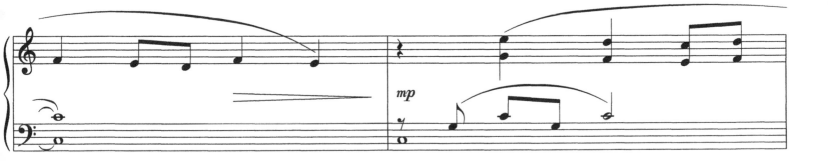

A WHOLE NEW WORLD
(ALADDIN'S THEME)
from Walt Disney's ALADDIN

Music by ALAN MENKEN
Lyrics by TIM RICE

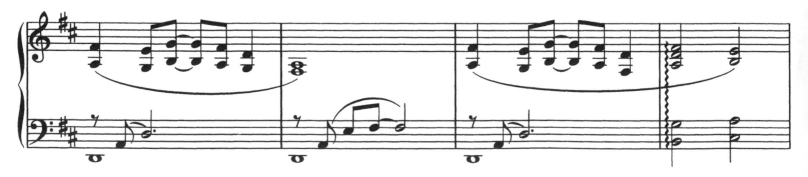

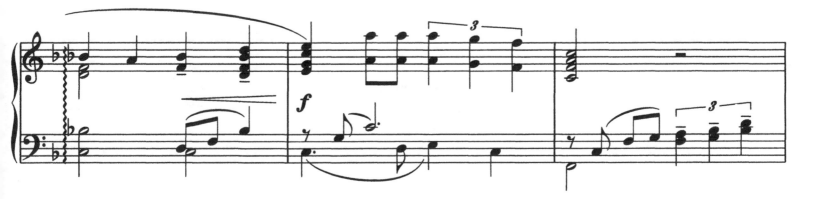